I CHOOSE
to Calm My Anger

I CHOOSE SERIES

ELIZABETH ESTRADA

I CHOOSE
to Calm My Anger

DEDICATED TO B.L.

ELIZABETH ESTRADA

I was angry at my mom and **dad**,
My parents said, "No," which made me **mad**.
I asked to play games with Aiden my best **friend**,
But chores after school were the rules, and wouldn't **bend**.

I begged, but no reason I could **find**
Could change my parents' **mind**.
I walked to school, a frown on my **face**,
I kicked a can and sent it to **space**.

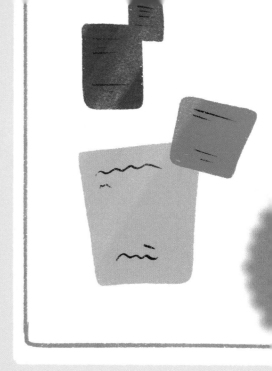

I went to my class, sat in the back of the **room**.
I just couldn't concentrate, I was so full of **gloom**.
A new boy sat near me and said, "Hi, I'm **Ray**.
I snapped at him and said, "Not **today**!"

At recess my friend, Liam, asked me, "What's **wrong**?
"Life's not always easy, but we have to be **strong**."
I can't help it, I can feel the anger boiling inside **me**.
"It's okay to feel anger, keeping it inside can make you **unhappy**."

"Accepting anger is important if we want to control **it**.
Just take three deep breaths and you won't want to **hit**.
Then, count up to ten, and you'll show anger the **door**.
Think of a happy place, and you'll be calm once **more**."

So I thanked my friend for his **help**.
I decided to be stronger than anger **itself**.
I breathed in and out deeply, then counted to **ten**,
And thought of a happy place to find my **zen**.

This helped me feel calmer and my anger had **eased**,
I walked to the playground where I sometimes got **teased**.
This was part of the problem that made me get **cross**,
I was bullied by a kid whose nickname was "**Boss**."

The big kid approached me and called me a rude **name**,
I could have barked back, but anger I chose to **tame**.
Because I said nothing, the bully **ignored**.
Boss shrugged and moved on because he was **bored**.

I felt surprised that this approach **worked**,
I had defeated my anger and my spirits **perked**.
Then, when I found out I didn't get picked for the **team**.
My hands sweat, and my anger grew **steam**.

But then I remembered to breathe in and **out**.
After I counted to ten, I no longer wanted to **shout**.
I knew what to do when I couldn't get my **way**,
I can keep my cool, come what **may**.

I never knew I could control my **anger**.
Thanks to my friend for helping me become **stronger**.
I learned it's okay to be angry and upset, **too**.
But it's up to me on how I respond and what I **do**.

I am calm.

I can breathe.

CALM

When I am mindful, I am aware of my feelings. When I am aware, I can accept and then manage my emotions.

I can visualize.

HIGH FIVE BREATH

This tool helps you stay calm by slowly breathing in and out.

For adults and children both...

1

Starting at the outside edge of your thumb, breathe in and use your index finger to trace up to the top. When you breathe out, slowly trace down the other side.

2

Keep breathing in and out, tracing up and down for a total of five breaths.

Keep going up and down until you reach the other side of your hand.

Begin here, at the outer edge of your thumb.

Dear Reader,

Thank you for reading my book. I hope you enjoyed a "I Choose to Calm My Anger." I spent fifteen years piecing together resources and ideas to help young children cope with big emotions.

So please tell me what you liked and even what you disliked. What kind of emotion should be in my next book?

I love to receive messages from my readers. Please write to me at Elizabethestradainfo@gmail.com

I would also greatly appreciate it if you could review my book.
Your feedback matters a lot to me!

With love,
Elizabeth

64044619R20021